MW00939111

Whispers From the Heart:

Daily Prayers For When the Flame is Flickering

Chris Altrock

Whispers From the Heart:
Daily Prayers For When the Flame is Flickering
Chris Altrock
2023
ISBN: 9798866797417
Imprint: Independently published

Prayers

for

(Re)starting

Love

#1: Into Your Hands

O Lord, in your heart
you carry me constantly.

And so into your hands
I commit myself completely.

I surrender to you not only
all that is
painful
to me.

I surrender to you also
all that is
precious
to me.

Into your hands I give it all.

#2: Un-alone

God,
because of you,
never
have I ever
been alone.

Always and forever
have I been
un-alone.

God,
because of you,
not once
have I ever been
unaided.

And thus, with You God,
always and forever
shall I be
unafraid.

#3: Open My Eyes

O God,
open my eyes
to see that

wherever I've been,
you are;

wherever I am,
you are;

and wherever I'm going,
you are.

#4: Author Above

Author above,
each time I review
the Book of
My Life,
may I read it as
a Book of
Our Life,
a story as much about *You*
as it is about *Me*.

#5: Fearfully and Wonderfully Made

O Creator,
attune my ears not
to the disdain of any who
raise me,
teach me,
loathe me,
lead me,
follow
or friend me.

Instead
attune my ears
only to the acclaim
of You who
made me and
saved me.

Help me, I pray,
know that truly I am
fearfully and wonderfully made.

#6: Holy Handiwork

Help me, O God,
to treat myself,
and every human,
as your holy handiwork,
people whom
you loved into living,
each your likeness and image.

#7: Mother Bear

O God, enlighten me
that I may know you as
Savior,
Son and
Spirit;

Creator,
Cornerstone and
Counselor;

Mother Bear,
Bridegroom and
Burning Fire;

Abba,
Advocate and
Almighty;

Love,
Lion and
Life;

and any other way
you choose to reveal
yourself to me.

#8: Be For Us Today

O God,
be for us this day
a faithful Giver,

a merciful Forgiver and

a powerful Deliverer.

#9: Soul Deep Satisfaction

O God,
may I never stop
seeking
the soul-deep
satisfaction
that only comes
through
savoring your steadfast
love.

#10: Everything and Nothing

With you,
beloved Christ,
I have everything,
even when I have
nothing.

Without you,
beloved Christ,
I have nothing,
even when I have
everything.

I cling tightly
to your love and
hold lightly
to all else.

#11: How Near You Are

Deliver me,
O God,
from the fallacy
of how far
from me you are,
because of how far
from you I feel.

Deliver me,
O God,
into the reality
of how near
you are to me,
and how beloved
I am by you,
regardless of how
I feel.

#12: Devotion

Beloved Christ,

like the devotion
shared by
a groom and a bride,

may the devotion
shared by
you and I

realign my
dreams and desires,

so that your passion
is all I ever pursue.

#13: More Than Love

Lord,
let my lips
confess,

and let my life
express,

this truth from Above,

that nothing matters
more than love.

#14: Finish Well

O God,
may the way I long
to conclude
my day

shape the entire
course of
my day.

May the impact I hope
I will have made

inspire a love
that I now display.

May my desire
to finish well
lead me now
to do well.

#15: Love Alone

Lord,
may love alone
be all I ever own;

my tick and my tock,

my do and don't,

my will and won't.

#16: Unmute Me

They command me,
"Shut up!"

You coax me,
"Speak up!"

They demand
my silence.

You desire
my story.

In unmuting me,
You, O God, unbind me.

#17: Enough

Could it be enough today,
dear Jesus,

to produce nothing
for you,

to present nothing
to you,

but to simply
be
with you?

#18: Help Me See Me

Jesus,
help me
see me.

Not the me
the doubter in me
or the haters near me
see in me.

Help me see
the me
You see.

The me
with all
the glory
and beauty
and majesty.

Prayers

for

When

We

Struggle

to

Love

#19: Coming Home

I'm coming home.

Once more I've wandered,
concluding that I need
what I want
more than I need
who You are,
more than I need
who I am
when I am
where You are.

I've accepted as truth
the lies of a life
apart from you.

I've accepted as lies
the truth of a life
alongside you.

But I've finally
come back to my senses.

And now I'm coming back to you,
despite what I think of me,
despite what people think of me,
because all that matters
is what you think of me.

I'm coming home.

#20: Lift Us O Lord

From the poison
of our partisanship,
lift us O Lord.

From the lethality
of our legalism,
lift us O Lord.

From our harshness
and hatefulness,
lift us O Lord.

From our ostracizing
and othering,
lift us O Lord.

Raise us,
resurrect us,
take from us
the grave clothes
of our inhumanity
and drape on us
the glorious clothes
of your divinity.

So that we may no longer
foment hell on earth,
but may instead
foster heaven on earth,
lift us O Lord.

#21: Tailor Made

Help me, Holy Spirit.

It's time we tossed out
these old threads.

Too long have I complied
with these clothes chosen
for me by others:

"Look like this,"
"Think like this,"
"Believe like this,"
"Behave like this."

No more.

I'm going to dress in
what you've
tailor-made
rather than in
what they've
mass-produced.

Holy Spirit, help me
get changed.
Help me look
more like you,
and, in so doing,
look more like myself.

#22: Someone Like Me

Jesus,
when I am with you,
I am so much more
than my many mistakes.

I am who I am
rather than just who I was.

There's never been
someone like you,

who treats me as if
there's never been
someone like me.

#23: Fractured

I hold in my hands
my heart,
O God.

It's all that's left
after the trainwrecks
of my mistakes.

Its fractured fragments
are broken
but still beating.

It's all I really have
for you.

But I know
it's all you really want
from me.

#24: Have Mercy

Lord, have mercy,
for we crave comparison
more than confession.

We lift ourselves up
by tearing others down.

We relish inquisition
of others
rather than introspection
of ourselves.

We delight in thinking how
they aren't as good as us
and we're not as bad as them.

Lord, have mercy,
so that we, too,
might learn to have mercy.

#25: Liberate My Love

May I no longer
focus on
who others are
and thus limit
my love to them.

May I, instead,
focus on
who I am
and thus liberate
my love for all.

#26: Let Go

God,
I finally realized
that the struggle
that just won't
let me go

is mostly a struggle
because I won't
let it go.

#27: Rock Free

God grant me
a rock free piety.

Let no stone remain
that I could aim
and cause pain
in your Name.

Remove all debris
reserved by me
including what
I've held back
to even hurt me.

#28: Begin Within

Help me do the work, Lord.

Not just the visible
exterior work,
but the invisible
interior work.

Not just clearing
my complexion
or improving
my clothes selection.

Aid me with
self-exploration
and self-revelation.

Accompany me
to my inner child
and my shadow self.

Embolden me to face
my hidden hurts,
buried beliefs and
masked memories.

Partner with me in
celebrating
what is healthy about me,
and repairing
all that is broken about me.

I want to begin within.

#29: The Salve That Saves Us

Let your love, O Christ,
heal
our
epidemic of exclusion,
our
disorder of division,
our
virus of violence,
our
illness of intolerance,
our
sickness of selfishness and
our
affliction of animosity.

Be the salve
that saves us
from ourselves.

#30: We

At the end,
may my life
and love
demonstrate
that what
mattered most
to me
was not *me*,
but *we*.

#31: Vision

Be thou my vision,
O Christ,

that I may no longer
be so observant
of all that
doesn't need to
concern me

and
so oblivious
to all that
should
concern me.

#32: A, B, C

1,
2,
3.
A,
B,
C.
Honestly,
completely,
I confess
each of my
iniquities.

1,
2,
3.
A,
B,
C.
From each one,
I am
finally,
fully,
set free,
by Your
mercy.

#33: Your Yes

God,

Your YES is
so much larger
than I dreamed
it could be.

Your NO is
so much smaller
than I dreaded
it would be.

Help me live
in this freedom
of what
you've actually said.

Not in the nightmare
of what
so many have said
you've said.

#34: Beauty From Blemishes

I seek not beauty
apart from my blemishes,
but beauty that comes
because of my blemishes.

I ask not for strength
from my weaknesses,
but for the strength
that comes through
my weaknesses.

I ask for the grace
to love and not loathe
all that seems to limit me.

For I am yours, O Christ.
You are the One who rose
from that tomb
scarred, not spotless,
flawed, not flawless,
magnificent in your
disfigurement.

#35: Rotten Roots

Help me, God,
not only with the
destructive deeds
that grieve my life,

but with the
disordered desires
that give them life.

Excavate these
rotten roots
that bear my
poison fruit.

#36: Lavish with Love

Lavish with love
Lord let me be.

For when love lives
in poverty,
I think obsessively
of the smallest wrongs
enacted against me.

But when love lives
in plenty,
I release freely
even the largest of wrongs
executed against me.

#37: Free Me

Jesus
free me,
from their thoughts
about me
that
haunt me and
hurt me.

Free me,
from all their
biases
about me
and bullying
of me.

Free me
to be fully,
fearlessly,
flourishingly,
courageously,
me.

Prayers

That

Give

Birth

to

Love

#38: Where Mary Started

God,
I'm not there yet.

But I want to
wind up
where Mary
started up.

I hunger for a heart
that says,
"I will do it,"

even when
my mind
still says,
"I don't
understand it."

#39: With Us

Immanuel,
thank you

for coming
to us

in a way that
convinces us

that even
when it feels like
God has
left us,

we can still be certain
that God is
with us.

#40: Sleep

God,
Jesus might have died,
if Joseph didn't sleep,
and in his sleep have dreams,
and in his dreams hear You,
and from that hearing act,
as only he could act,
to save Jesus
from Herod.

And it makes me wonder,
how we don't act,
because we don't hear,
because we don't dream,
because we just won't sleep.

#41: Lifted and Lowered

Lord,
let me be part
of how your love
lifts
those lowered
by others,
and
lowers
those lifted
by themselves.

#42: Manger Community

Thank you Jesus
for drawing near
to us through
the peril of birth,
the powerlessness of
swaddling clothes and
the homelessness of a manger.

Make us a
birthing-community,
enduring danger
to draw near to others.

Make us a
swaddling-community,
wrapping in warmth
all who are without.

Make us a
manger-community,
welcoming home all
who are homeless.

#43: Lunar God

Lauds and Daytime
have long been
my prayers to you,
believing that
as a Solar God,
you are
most active
under the sun.

But may
Vespers and Compline
also become
my prayer to you,
believing that
as a Lunar God
you are
as active at night
as you are in the light.

#44: Present

Christ,
may I not join the many
who are so preoccupied
that they
simply pass by
all your presents this day.

May I,
like Mary,
be present
to all you provide,
and pause to ponder
their worth
and savor
their significance.

#45: Rising Up, Bowing Down

O' Little Child of Bethlehem,
half of me,
like Herod,
rises up
at your birth.
I dread
you taking charge
of all I crave to control.

The rest of me,
like magi,
bows down
at your birth.
I delight in
you taking charge
of all I cannot control.

May delight
defeat dread
as I enter
your dominion.

#46: Adoration and Affliction

Lord Jesus,
in one
magnificent and
messy moment
you were given
all at once
to your mother Mary.

And then,
over twelve thousand
delightful and
distressing days,
you were taken
piece by piece
from your mother Mary.

Long before spikes
pierced your flesh,
a sword pierced her soul.
Your Advent filled her holy heart
with adoration and affliction.

May we whose hearts beat
with similarly mixed rhythms
find in her
our traveling companion.

#47: Mother of Sorrows

Lord Jesus,
Mary became
the Mother of Sorrows
in order to become
the Mother of the Savior.

May I too
embrace any pain
that is required
by my passion for you.

#48: Joy and Thanks

Lord Jesus,
when you
descended to us,
we found Anna
worshiping
day and night in the temple.

Lord Jesus,
when you
ascended from us,
we found your disciples
worshiping
continually in the temple.

Your time with us
began and ended
with endless praise.

Likewise,
may your ongoing presence
with us
ignite a flame of
joy and thanks
in us
that no day
will ever douse
and no experience
will ever extinguish.

#49: Wonder and Weeping

Christ,
at your coming,
you made room
not only for
wonder
but also for
weeping.

May I too find
a home for
heartbreak--
mine,
yours
and that of all who,
like you,
face days with loss
not just laughter.

#50: Nazareth

Jesus,
your childhood
begins and ends
in Nazareth.

From cradle to cross,
you were called
"Jesus of Nazareth."

You found yourself
among the forgotten,
not the famous.

May I, too,
find myself among
nobodies and nowheres.

May I learn to be content
with my own Nazareth.

#51: New

Lord Jesus,
as I face
a new year,
a new opportunity,
a new challenge,
or a new chance,

replace
within me
a self
that serves
so that
I might be loved

with a self
that serves
because
I am already loved.

#52: It is Time

Lord Jesus,

before I head into
a new year,
a new opportunity,
a new challenge,
a new chance,

help me
to first leave
my Nazareth,

knowing,
just as you did
upon your departure,
that "It is time."

#53: A Chance to Surrender

Jesus,

let every new chapter
be a new chance

to surrender
to what you want most

rather than to secure
what I want most;

to give to others
rather than to gain for myself;

to further your dreams
rather than to fulfill my desires.

#54: Prayerfulness

Lord Jesus,

your three years of
transformative ministry

for God

began with an
entire night in prayer

to God.

Remind me constantly
that fulfilling my own desire
for years of fruitfulness

for you

will depend on
hours of prayerfulness

with you.

#55: Constant Companion

Thank you, Jesus, for being a
constant companion.

Grant me courage
to embrace the way
your companionship comes
through the flesh and blood of others.

Enlighten me to see how
doing life
with them today
is doing life
with you today.

#56 A Posture of Proximity

Grant me courage,
Lord Jesus,
to adopt a
posture of proximity
to those most in need of
what I can provide.

Help me to leave safe havens
to come alongside
hurting people.

Prayers

for

When

Love

Hurts

#57: Love and Die

O Christ,
I wish I could
cherish others
better
without being
hurt so
badly.

Nevertheless,
because I long to love
like you do,
I ask you to help me
love, and live,
and die,
as you do.

#58: Daring Enough

Jesus, help me walk
the Way of Love

even if this act
only attracts
people who wish
to attack,

even if your Way
only scares away
people I wish
would stay.

Make me daring enough
to always do
what your love demands.

#59: Advance

Christ,
may no word
spoken
against me

and no wound
inflicted
upon me

arrest my
advance
along your
Way of Love.

#60: Seen

Jesus, turn and look
upon me this day.
If I can just be seen,
truly seen,
by you,
I won't need to be seen
by any other.

Even in my
messiest moments,
grant me
your look of love.

And then
empower me
to offer this same
gift to others.

May all who
are unseen
and mis-seen
know they are
truly seen
and fully seen
by you,
and
by me.

#61: Calm and Quiet

Jesus,
calm and quiet
my soul.

May I not add the words of
hate, hurt and horror
within me
as fuel for the flames
others have ignited
around me.

Instead, let my words be few.

May my silence reflect
a heart
centered in and
surrendered to
you.

Jesus,
calm and quiet
my soul.

#62 Labels

Jesus,
may all people
experience
love
from me

even if
it means
some people
place labels
on me.

May their
little or large labels
never limit
my love.

#63: Behold

Jesus,

I
behold
much that is
hard to hold.

From the disquieting news
in the headlines,
to the discouraging voices
in my head
to the disappointments
held in my heart.

I
behold
much that is
hard to hold.

I
beg you to let me
behold

you,

and in so doing,
to see more clearly
all else that
I
behold.

#64: Burdens

Savior,
grant me compassion
to weep for all the burdens
others carry today
along this road.

Grant me courage
to bear and share
at least some
of the burdens myself.

#65: Open Wound

Jesus,
if I must bear this
painful wound,

may it at least become an
open wound—

the kind that opens my sight to
the suffering of others

rather than just
the misery of me.

#66: Testimony

Jesus,
I see what they've
said about you,

scrawled on that
sign above you.

The pronouncement
of the powerful.

So, I'm climbing your cross,
because I've got my own
placard to post.

My testimony
to your
mercy,
charity,
empathy,
clarity,
humanity,
and glory.

#67: The End

Jesus,

I've reached
the end of a road

and

the end of my rope.

Here,
in this place of endings,
let me find you.

And let me be found by you.

#68: Remembered

I've often
forgotten
the many
who need to be
remembered.

But you Jesus
have always
remembered
the many
who have been
forgotten—

or who, like me, are
forgetting.

#69: Crucified Community

Jesus,
at the foot of your cross,
baptized by the
blood of your wounds,

we have found
a crucified community,
a house for the hurting.

Thank you for making
this space for us,
where we can
hurt and heal
together.

#70: It Matters

Dear God,
I hate to bother you
with this.
It might look small
in the face of bigger things.
Still, this small thing feels
like a big thing
to me
and I don't know what else to do
about it,
but come and talk to you
about it.
I trust that
you think it matters,
simply because
I think it matters.

#71: Why?!

Why?!

I don't understand it.
And I will never forget it.

Why
on earth
would You
allow this to happen?

Where
on earth
were You
when it happened?

I feel like
You're lounging there
in your Heaven.

While
I'm languishing here
in this Hell.

And I'd like just one word
with You:

Why?!

#72: Release

Jesus,
help me,

like you,

release all that I carry--

every care and concern--

into the hands
of our Father.

#73: Done

Dear God,
I'm done.

In
more
ways
than
one.

#74: Wound

O Christ,
like Eve,

I am (re) born
by the life unleashed
by the wound in your side.

Like the woman at the well,

I am filled
with the Spirit that flows
by the wound in your side.

Like Peter,

I am welcomed back,
again and again,
at the table initiated
by the wound in your side.

#75: There

Lord Jesus,
you're there

when everything
has ended

and you're there
before anything
has started.

Prayers

for

Love

to

Triumph

#76: New Love

Living One,

I've come
to this space,
dreading
that I'll
discover
the death
of an old hope,
plan or
expectation.

Open my eyes
(and my imagination)
that I might instead see
the new life
and new love
made possible
only by your power.

#77: Mad Hope

Risen One,
I want to

believe in hope,

and bear hope,

so strongly,
so stubbornly,

that others think
I've turned and gone

stark raving mad.

#78: Present Absence

Jesus,
grant me the capacity
to rest comfortably
in your presence,
even in spaces
that only seem to prove
your absence.

#79: Spark

Jesus,
may the hope
you've rekindled

in the heart
within me

become the ember
which sparks

the heart
next to me.

#80: Stay

Jesus,
will you stay
with me?

Humans and hope
have receded
like the tide.

People and promises
have all
turned aside.

Jesus,
will *you* stay
with me?

#81: Locked Doors

Dear Jesus,

as I sit,
once again,
behind
locked doors,

show me
enough of you
in here

to overcome
my fear of what's
out there.

#82: Follow Me

Jesus,

I said
I'd follow you
wherever you went.

And then I couldn't.

Or wouldn't.

And I didn't.

But now I'm wondering.

Now that I'm in this
place of regret.
Remorse.
Reproach.

Could you.
Would you.
Still follow me?

#83: You Made Me

I should have gone
straight to you, Jesus,
in the aftermath of my
awfulness.

Instead, you've come
straight to me.

As you did with Peter,
you've come not
requiring me to
rehearse my failure
against you,
against you,
against you.

Instead, you've come
rousing me to
remember my fervor
for you,
for you,
for you.

You've come not to expose
the beastly human
I believe my mistakes
have made me.

You've come to affirm
the beloved human
I can't believe my Messiah
has made me.

#84: Cascade

Holy Spirit,
flow upon me.

Cascade over my
mind and mouth,
heart and hands,
down even to my feet—
top to bottom.

Let your torrent transform
my logic and language,
my passion and my power,
my entire direction.

Only then will I be able to
give up my plans
to create a kingdom for myself,

and take up your plans
to create a kingdom for all.

#85: Blow and Burn

Holy Spirit, blow.
Inspire us.

Holy Spirit, burn.
Rekindle us.

Draw us into your dream
of a world that's finally one.

Let your breath restore
every bridge we've razed.

Let your blaze ruin
every barrier we've raised.

#86: Fire

Come Holy Spirit,
be the flame of fire
that refines this world.

Scorch and torch
every sin
of injustice and inequity--
all the way to the ground.

And then come Holy Spirit,
be the flow of water,
that refreshes this world.

Nourish and flourish
the seeds
of freedom and justice--
in the rich soil that remains.

#87: Feast

Since we are what we eat,
then let us feast,
Holy Spirit,
on your fruit.

Our skeletal souls pine
for your produce.

Let the juice and pulp
of every one of your
tasty types of love
drip
down
our
chins

and fill our famished selves.

Renew us,
restore us,
remake us
from the inside out.

#88: Speak

Holy Spirit,
I once was taught
that you once spoke,
but that your counsel
has ceased,
found now only in
ancient Scripture,
your mighty voice muted.

But when I read that
same Scripture,
it taught me
that you still speak,
and that your counsel
is continuous,
experienced through
your indwelling presence,
your striking voice
still sounding,
every day in my soul and
my surroundings.

So speak, Spirit,
for your servant is listening.

#89: Breathe

Breathe,
Holy Spirit,
breathe.

Expand my
exhausted lungs,
and I'll get my
second wind.

Stir,
Holy Spirit,
stir.

Cool my
sweltering soul,
and I'll step back
in the game.

Blow,
Holy Spirit,
blow.

Fill my
rumpled sails,
and I'll fly
across the water

wherever you want
me to go

#90: Whole House

Holy Spirit,
I want my soul
so full of you,
that I'm like

a show
with standing
room only,

a river
with flood-waters,
still rising,

a rush hour train
without a single
seat available.

I don't want you moving in
and just taking
a guest room as yours.

I want you making
the whole house yours.

#91: My Ceaseless Sunday

Spirit of God,
I choose to believe that your
indwelling of me
means there is something
immortal about me.

I may be
knocked down,
or knocked out,

but
no malice or malevolence,
prejudice or pain
can truly take me out.

Despite my frequent
Good Fridays,
you are
my ceaseless Sunday.

#92: Family

Spirit of God,
work relentlessly
to assure me
that I'm more than
a day laborer to God—

remind me
that I'm a child of God;

especially when prodigal-me
returns so pitifully
from a far away land,

hoping just to be
God's next hired hand.

In those seasons
when I expect the very least,

remind me of my place
at the Father's feast.

Remind me that I am now,
and forever will be,
God's own family.

#93: Loving with Heart

Thank you Jesus
for a love
that involves
your entire *heart*.

You love so deeply
even when it costs
so dearly.

The constancy of fervor
from you
brings me constantly back
to you.

Forgive me for times
when I've been half-hearted,
when I've held back
parts of my heart
from you and others,
when my own devotion
has not beaten
as loudly as your own.

Grant me the ability
to live and love
whole-heartedly,
to be emotionally available to
myself, you and others.

May my every day
pulse with passion.

#94: Loving with Soul

Thank you Jesus for loving me
and so many others
with all your *soul*,

for a love that is
not superficial
or merely external,
but that emanates
from your very core.

Forgive me for times
when my own love
for you or others
has been skin-deep
and lightweight.

Grant me the ability to love
from the inside out,
to have a dedication that is
authentic and genuine,
through and through.

#95: Loving with Mind

Thank you Jesus
for loving me
and so many others
with all your *mind*;

for the ways you are
so attentive to us
and
so thoughtful of us.

Forgive me for times
when I've been preoccupied
with so much
that I was thoughtless
or forgetful of so many,
including you.

Grant me the ability
to think good things
of you and of others,
to be mindful of you and them
at all times.

#96: Loving with Strength

Thank you Jesus
for loving me
and so many others
in a way that engaged
all your *strength*—

your talents,
abilities,
energy,
resources and
even your body.

Forgive me for times
when my own love is
weak and anemic;
reserved or compartmentalized;
for my misuse or even abuse
of my own gifts,
energy and body.

Grant me the ability to love
all--myself included—
with tenacity and resilience;
to marshal everything I have and am
for the good of God and others.

#97: Loving Your Neighbor

Thank you Jesus
for a love that envelopes
every *neighbor*,
even me.

Thank you for
enlarging neighbor
so that it
includes all and excludes none.

Forgive me for times
when I've narrowed
that definition
and reserved my love
only for those like me.

Grant me the capacity
to tear down those walls
and let love loose,
to love my neighbor
as I love myself,
no matter who that neighbor is.

#98: Not Alone

I am *not* alone.

Here, at the cross,
I find solidarity with
the Crucified One.
Here, at the cross,
I find solidarity with
his crucified ones.

I am linked with all
who have ever lamented.

I am bound with all
who have ever been broken.

Jesus folds me into
a forsaken family.

I am not alone.

#99: Three Stages

O God of the Ages.
O God of Three Stages.

You twice heard the
praying people of God.
You twice unleashed the
powerful Spirit of God.

We've read the history
of this bi-fold movement.
Stage One and Stage Two.
Reaching both Gentile and Jew.

O God, let us now make new history.
Let us now be Stage Three.
Reaching across all land and sea.

Through our appeals today
unleash the Spirit we pray.
Like the fires of a rocket engine,
Let us be the light
that shines through the generations.

#100: Into Your Hands (Again)

O Lord, in your heart
you carry me constantly.

And so into your hands
I commit myself completely.

I surrender to you not only
all that is painful to me.
I surrender to you also
all that is precious to me.

Into your hands I give it all.

Made in United States
Orlando, FL
28 November 2023

39709982R00061